Mirror, Mirror, on the Wall . . .

Where Does My Self-Love Fall?

A Success Guide to Replace Toxicity with Love

Nina Norstrom

Virginia

Mirror, Mirror, on the Wall . . . Where Does My Self-Love Fall? A Success Guide to Replace Toxicity with Love

A portion of the proceeds will go to help fund the fight against toxic relationships.

Published in the United States by Writelife Publishing
www.writelife.com
(an imprint of Boutique of Quality Books Publishing, Inc.)

Printed in the United States of America

978-1-60808-195-0 (p)
978-1-60808-196-7 (e)

Library of Congress Control Number: 2018951090
Book design by Robin Krauss, www.lindendesign.biz
Cover design by Marla Thompson, www.edgeofwater.com

First editor: Olivia Swenson
Second editor: Caleb Guard

"Hand Gestures Hand Drawn" from Vecteezy, www.vecteezy.com

Praise for Mirror, Mirror, on the Wall...

"If you have experienced toxicity in your relationships in life, this book will provide you a guide to successfully replace your toxicity with love for self and others."

—Dr. Prentis V. Johnson, PhD, ThD
Founder/Chancellor, Agape Bible College

"Self-love is the basis of all emotional healing. In this book, Nina Norstrom guides readers through an engaging and life-affirming journey."

—Tim Desmond, author of *The Self-Compassion Skills Workbook*

A Specialty Gift

From: _____

This guide is presented to _____

On this day, _____

My special message:

Contents at a Glance

Heartfelt Gratitude

There's so much love and thought wrapped in these pages to benefit you, the reader. I'd like to acknowledge and extend a heartfelt thank you to the following individuals who have helped make this product a valuable resource:

To the professionals who assisted in the editing and proofing phases of this literary production, I extend my gratitude. Also, praise and appreciation goes to all who contributed their thoughts and feedback for the topic of "Young Adults Dating-N-Violence."

To my wonderful publisher, Terri Leidich, for believing in the material. Her support and the support of her staff was greatly appreciated.

To all readers who embrace and purchase this creation, I offer a gracious and warm thank you! None of this would have been possible without the assistance and support from *everyone* involved.

Self-Love: What Is It?

You can't look for something when you don't know what to look for . . .

Self-love is not an item you can purchase. All the money in the world can't buy self-love. You can take a shovel and dig a hole in the ground all day, but you will never find the thing called self-love. It's something you must possess within yourself.

Self-Love:

1) Self-love is not only a concept, but a mindset. Think of the term as having unconditional love for self—a love like no other human can provide, a love for the skin that you are in.

2) Self-love involves nurturing yourself by giving unconditional (spoiling) love to yourself and ensuring that you maintain a life of wellness. Part of self-care is not allowing anyone to ever take advantage of or disregard you.

3) Self-love is visible in the actions you take to increase your love of self.

How Does Self-Love Appear?

Self-love can appear in a myriad of ways. Listed below are just a few. Add your own self-loving actions to the list.

- Speaking what's on your mind in a respectful, caring way.
- Making daily choices for your benefit.
- When feeling overworked, taking time to slow down and relax. And not starting again until you feel reenergized.
- Indulging in a bath filled with your favorite bubble bath or essential oils.

Preparatory Section

Through My Own Eyes: Discovery

Take a mental step out of the box as we prepare for and embrace all forthcoming material.

Before you take the challenge to read this guide, it helps to explore your world in all its existing elements. Our physical world is our planet and all the living entities it sustains. All varieties of trees, flowers, and animals thrive in its many habitats. We can even break each aspect of our world into its component parts— elements, atoms, metals, and minerals. But your personal world goes beyond your physical surroundings of sky, moon, and  ground, beyond your molecular makeup. No one can tell you how to view your world— only you have that vision. *It's your world!* So, in your present mindset, how do you perceive it? Take into account your inner aspect being made up of emotions and feelings.

EXERCISE

Suggested material for use: pencil/pen, colored pencils/crayons.

This exercise is an opportunity to draw and add color to the concept of your worldview using colored pencils, crayons, pencil, and/or pen. You could depict your worldview through a literal drawing of your physical surroundings and actual faces for your emotions or a metaphorical drawing where colors and shapes represent your world. You may want to label the elements or make a code (trees = green; mate or partner = brown or pink; anger = black, etc.). Don't think too hard. There's no perfect way to do this! Let your mind create the world it sees. As a comparison, you'll do another drawing of your worldview at the conclusion of this guide. Now, start the artwork and color your world.

Introduction

What Ya Got for Me?

Welcome! Life throws many curves into one's pathway. How one handles those curves creates the beauty of the journey. This guide is meant for everyone. Anyone eager to satisfy their hunger and thirst to find self-love and remove toxic relationships will benefit from its use.

The guide has a dual purpose: developing self-love and creating awareness of toxic relationships. To direct you toward those purposes, this guide is equipped with information and activities that require daily thought and participation. You'll discover there is a lot to absorb and focus on. Consider taking frequent breaks to get recharged and energized for the coming of a new you! All chapters contain information as well as activities that help you apply what you've learned. Don't dismiss or shy away from the information sections. Knowledge is power, especially when that knowledge gives you the freedom to engage and empower yourself. This guide's information is part of a discovery for finding self-love and exposing the ugliness of toxicity. Embrace it, remember it, and practice it! Internalizing the information and participating in the activities outlined will maximize your success.

There aren't right or wrong answers for this guide. What's important is the opportunity to flush out your thoughts, realize the makeup of your relationship(s), discover toxicity with its many faces in your life, decide how you will react to the toxicity, and embrace the pure self-love you deserve. Once you've acknowledged the truth about "self," there should be no turning back. With these goals in mind, there was no need to insert an answer key for any of the working activities. The "master key" lies within you.

Unlocking the answers you seek will depend on how you respond to the information and activities in this guide and how well you handle the self-realization that will accompany those responses. Dig deep and examine the layers of self that reside within your being. Absorbing the information will help you discover and respond to the toxicity that exists within your circle.

Before diving in, think about this question:

How much do you love yourself?

Loving yourself comes before loving another. The belief you're unlovable hinders your ability to open the gateway to love and forgive. Self-forgiveness, self-acceptance, self-compassion, self-confidence, self-worth, self-esteem, self-love—all these dimensions are essential to develop in your emotional healing process.

A few practical notes: Lined or blank pages have been inserted after activities that require one or the other. Feel free to purchase an inexpensive notebook as a larger companion for this guide. A few activities call for colored pencils or crayons. For the writing exercises, don't focus on grammar, spelling, punctuation, or sentence structure. Just put it down and get it out. It's more important to let go of the stress that weighs you down.

Now, it's time to find out where your footprints will lead. Take a deep breath and then exhale. Let's do that again—inhale and exhale. The fun begins . . .

Ready, set, go!

Reflect on . . .

This preparatory section gives you a chance to reflect on your current understanding of three key aspects of self-love and awareness of toxic relationships. Feel free to think about the answers to the questions or record your thoughts on the pages provided or in a separate notebook.

Healthy Relationships

After listening to a friend's story of a relationship, were you struck by his or her level of confidence, self-love, forgiveness, or awareness of a partner's negative actions (also known as a partner's toxicity)? It's often easier to identify these attributes in others than in ourselves. Take this opportunity to do a bit of reflection on your own relationships. How would others looking in view your relationships? Would they see a healthy relationship? What does a healthy relationship look like to you? What does it take to maintain a healthy relationship?

After reflecting on healthy relationships, consider the opposite—think about or record some brief details relating to an unhealthy relationship you've encountered.

Letting Go

You must be ready to let go of those parts of life holding you back or dragging you down, especially when it comes to relationships. Clinging to damaging relationships halts the growth process. Living inside an unhealthy past makes it difficult to embrace a new life. When we get stuck in painful memories, we're unable to enjoy and live a healthy lifestyle. We lose sight of the beauty that healing brings and are unable to learn from life's lessons. With experiences come new lessons; each new day is a gift from above. While clinging to the past, we delay obtaining those lessons. Can you think of anyone in your circle of friends, family, and acquaintances who was or is unable to let go of those unhealthy memories or moments? If so, how did the situation achieve a positive outcome? Use any instance (including self) to draw upon that reflection.

The key to letting go is being able to forgive yourself. Holding onto painful past events keeps the hurtful experience inside a negative space and does nothing to heal the wound. Consider the following statements and questions about letting go and forgiveness:

- How have you moved on from a relationship?

- Is there a painful past experience you need to be healed of?

- Write about a time you forgave and how it felt.

- Write a brief "healing scripture" or inspirational message one might use to overcome a tragedy or hardship.

- Using your imagination, how would you draw forgiveness and/or healing?

Confidence

To maximize self-love, one must acquire confidence. Can you identify some components or habits used to achieve lasting and unbreakable confidence? How do you see yourself in each component? Use the examples as a guide:

I identify self-esteem as a component of confidence, and my self-esteem is bolstered by the fact that I'm good at whatever I undertake. Self-reliance is another component; I make my own choices and take ownership of the consequences—doing so increases my confidence.

Using your imagination, how would you draw or color self-love?

1

Toxic Defined in the Raw

Identifying the Faces

It takes a great deal of work to build healthy relationships. Don't be discouraged as you make the effort. Anything that grows requires daily nurturing. In the process, be aware the word "toxic" exists. Toxicity has become a worldwide phenomenon and a visible reality among every aspect of today's society.

Raising one's awareness of toxicity is like shining a bright light directly into a dark room—the darkness flees and only light remains. Toxicity is made up of negative elements or entities of any sort that attach to our being and bring on an unhealthy interaction. The following statement could be a prime example of a negative entity image: *I thought I was over my depressive state but it still lingers*. These negative entities cannot survive inside purity. To shine the light on toxic relationships, one must embrace the *pure* essence of self-esteem, self-love, and self-confidence. Negative entities contaminate our ability to acquire self-esteem, self-confidence, and happiness, hindering our vision of the greatness that lives around us. Such contamination drains our energy and leaves us feeling listless. It can happen easily and quickly.

Toxicity in the context of a bigger stage, like today's society, is readily apparent. The negative entity that creeps inside our circle is usually masked in a variety of shapes, sizes, and disguises—all creating conflict and damage. When the conflict erupts, we see the unhealthiness clearly. These unhealthy interactions become readily visible when our soldiers are on the battlefield fighting a war, when fathers fight against their sons, when mothers turn against their daughters, in the abandonment of and cruelty to our animals, in our emotions soaring against our feelings, in the abuse of alcohol and drugs, in the ugliness of illnesses *and* diseases—the list goes on. These unhealthy interactions become the norm and begin to make up our own relationships.

Life is full of relationships, giving ample opportunity for toxicity to rear its ugly head and find a home. Think about the people in your immediate circle—those you see on a daily basis. Do your interactions with any of them make you feel ashamed, embarrassed, or negative? Then think about people in your broader circle—those you see on a weekly or monthly basis—and ask yourself the same question.

What are some other words that describe toxicity? Thinking of synonyms can help you identify toxic relationships where you didn't expect to see one. I call these other words the "faces" of toxicity because they identify all the different ways toxicity can appear in our lives. I'll start with a couple ideas, and then you can take it away from there. Let's have some fun!

Toxic makes me think of . . .

• Poison

• Raw

How many "faces" can you think of? Plenty more, I'm sure! Feel free to use bullet points to list your responses.

Now that you have the list, think about someone in your circle who fits one of the faces. What has made your interaction with them a toxic one? Were you initially aware of their disposition? How have you dealt with that person's toxicity?

Toxic Exposures

Let's take a more in-depth look at ways you can be exposed to toxicity from a relationship standpoint.

Different relationships in their many disguises can be toxic when involving:

- people (such as the boss-employee power struggle, colleague-colleague bullying, friend-friend verbal abuse, spouse-spouse manipulation, etc.)

- diseases or illnesses (such as the Ebola virus, cancer, addiction, or PTSD)

- emotions or feelings (such as rage, shame, worry, or bitterness)

Try to add to the list above, either as a new category or as examples of an existing category.

Challenge

Identify some of the ways we are exposed to toxicity by filling in the blank spaces.

a _ _ _ _ _ s, b _ _ _ _ _ _ _ _ _ _ s, d _ _ _ _ _ _ s, d _ _ _ s, e _ _ _ _ _ _ s,

r _ _ _ _ _ _ s, and e _ _ _ _ _ _ _ _ _ s.

Identifying Toxicity

It's extremely important to understand that toxic relationships occur regardless of one's sexual orientation. Living a healthy lifestyle shouldn't be a challenge. Yet we consistently engage in unhealthy relationships and situations. These questions will help you gauge your ability to identify those toxic relationships. We will discuss toxic relationships further in Section 7.

1) How does society define a toxic relationship?

2) Think about the unhealthy signs that signal toxicity in a romantic relationship. Name four of those signs. As you list them, describe what they look like inside the relationship. For example, abuse is a sign of toxicity and could look like one partner hitting the other, one partner calling the other ugly, or one partner telling the other, "No one will ever want you but me."

3) What is it about your relationships that require a change? You may want to define that change by starting with the following statements: I know I must . . .; I will remove/give up . . .

4) When you remove a toxic element from your life, you are left with free space. What would you like to add to that free space you've created? You may want to start with the following statement: I'm going to fill my free space with . . .

5) a. Identify one relationship from the past that was extremely unhealthy, damaging, and suffocating. Write a message to yourself or partner relaying why you've moved on. Do this with no holds barred and remain true to self.

b. It's important you *don't* keep toxicity among your precious possessions. After writing the message, find a way to destroy it. You can send it to a friend, family member, or church; throw it in the garbage; rip it to shreds; bury it; cut it up; or burn it up! It doesn't matter how you rid yourself of this poison . . . just remove it! After letting go of that negative entity, how does it feel? Be precise in your explanation. Tell it all—emotions, feelings, and overall satisfaction.

2

Letting Go to Rediscover Self

Every one of us will experience some form of a negative entity. This negativity isn't always the consequence of toxic relationships. There are other forms of toxicity to be considered—particularly within our own minds. These negative entities can be very damaging and harmful to our well-being. Cleansing one's life spiritually and emotionally is so refreshing. The discovery of self comes alive!

The journey of self-discovery is an ongoing process, a tough and rocky trail. As those emotions and surroundings are unveiled, the effects of self-discovery bring enlightenment, fulfillment, and clarity to your life. You begin to understand who you really are. While moving from one relationship to another, you give self space to heal. When you explore beneath the surface of yourself, the very essence of knowing your true being can open your eyes.

You and your partner may want to do things together as a unit, but don't lose yourself in the process. You'll be stumbling to find your way back. When you become a part of your partner and he/she becomes a replica of you, it won't be easy to see a clear picture of exactly who's who. Your thinking process vanishes and your identity disappears. Suddenly, you've become one and the same. You will have the same feelings and emotions, do the same things, say the same things, speak in the same manner, and act out the same way. In reality, you and your partner are different and separate people. It's important not to compromise your own identity for someone else, not even for romantic relationships or friends. Be true to yourself, and keep the inner you intact. Taking care of self may be a challenge, but think of it as a necessity.

Know when your identity has been stripped or lost. Otherwise, you won't recognize self. You have a life separate from your partner. No one can live it but you. Have you forgotten? You have your *own* identity . . . don't become a shadow of your partner. If one of you absorbs the other's identity, it will be difficult to define who the Absorber is. Just be aware it happens. When it does, you won't even realize it or know yourself. You'll have a misconception of who you are. *Self* is a big part of who you are. Embrace that self-love and keep it intact!

So often we find ourselves lost in relationships because we don't know ourselves. With this exercise, you'll peel back one layer of self at a time. When it's all over, you'll find yourself—you, the one that is beautiful and unique!

Consider the journey you've taken thus far, and discover a piece of you in these questions:

a) What do you *not* admire about yourself? State why you don't adore that characteristic.

b) What self-love habits do you possess? What are you doing to maintain those habits?

c) Make a list of your self-love desires/goals. In what order would you list them, starting with most important?

d) What obstacles do you face in acquiring self-love? List three adjustments you can make to overcome these obstacles.

e) Where are you in the process of obtaining self-love? Be honest with yourself, both about how far you have to go and how far you've come.

f) What about self makes you beautiful? Consider using the following statement to define your beauty: I am beautiful because of my . . .

g) We all have special qualities. What makes your qualities unique? Consider using the following statement to define that uniqueness: I am unique because . . .

Self or Selfish

This world is made up of all sorts of people. Regardless of their character and opinion of themselves, they are who they choose to be and deserve to be accepted. Are you at your best? Do you feel comfortable in your own skin? The most valuable and greatest relationship we'll have in life is with ourselves. It's important to remain true to one's self. We must be honest and forthright about who we are and how we perceive ourselves. Others, such as family, friends, and partners, may have their own perception of us and that's okay.

It takes dedication to "self-concepts" (self-confidence, self-love, etc.) to reach optimum satisfaction in life. Maybe you don't have the gall to stand up for what you know or like. You're comfortable in your shyness. You may like being a dependent and know you are needy. You may like being someone's punching bag. You may enjoy shedding tears. You may like hearing yourself speak and know you are a whiner. You may admire the way another person stands up for themselves. You may think having looks is more attractive than brains. You may think having pockets full of money will buy you a new image.

Sometimes, it's the truth about self that seems overly harsh or even becomes a hard pill to dissolve. The beauty of this life is feeling comfortable inside one's own skin. And that's what matters. This means accepting how poorly or negatively we see ourselves, how we look, how we think of ourselves, how we choose to describe ourselves, how we choose to act, and the value of having good self-esteem. It's important to know the value of one's self-esteem is measured by the positive or negative side of one's self-worth. When you're comfortable with self, you begin to embrace the world around you.

While there are many interesting and different people to be in life, I'd rather be myself. I have come to love this new me that lives inside my skin. My journey has been very enriching and fulfilling. With a new vision of who I am in hand, I've come to admire and embrace my self-concepts. I cannot imagine anything more rewarding than meeting wonderful people, appreciating the beauty of life, and exploring and experiencing all the wonders life has to offer. To be able to care about others, share knowledge, and have compassion—there is nothing like the enjoyment of it all. What a great life I have, and you can have too as you accept self! There are so many more wonders to life that makes me want to remain who I am. With all my qualities for kindness, friendliness, caring, and dependability, and more, I just love being me! Remember, a person's first impression of you will last. Don't be afraid to show the world the real you. Self can be beautiful when it's you!

EXERCISE

If you could be someone other than yourself, who would you want to be? This could be a celebrity, a family member, or a friend. Perhaps you choose to remain as you are—yourself. Think out your reasoning clearly and you'll be surprised by the discoveries you have about self.

Put Your Mask on First

First and foremost, help yourself before taking care of others. Remember the words from every flight safety video: *Before you assist anyone, always make sure your own oxygen mask is secured.* This is so true! How can you help someone if your situation is in jeopardy or unstable? If you're not conscious of your own safety, the likelihood of survival is limited. Put your mask on first! What does this mean in regard to self? There are many ways one can take care of self and thereby condition themselves to nurture others. Some ways to take care of self include staying healthy in mind and body, avoiding drama, and being a peacemaker. What are some other ways you can take care of self?

Nurturing Self

Did you know self-nurture and self-care are core parts of who you are? When you begin to self-nurture, you're caring for self. Just as you have to put your mask on first, you will have to love yourself to practice self-care. Self-care is priceless and should be a top priority on any to-do list. When self-nurturing and self-caring come together, you've internally validated self. Consider relaxation a formula for one's physical and emotional wellness.

There are a variety of ways one nurtures and cares for self, but generally the activity should be done alone to focus on self. These are some simple suggestions:

- Do some mediation while relaxing mind, body, and soul
- Get your eyebrows trimmed or waxed
- Have a hand and foot massage
- Listen to your favorite music
- Pop in a movie and indulge with popcorn or chips
- See a play
- Spend time at the gym working on self
- Spend the day at the beach
- Stay in your pajamas and indulge with strawberries and whipped cream
- Take a nice long hot and soapy bubbly bath with a few scented candles around the tub
- Take a nice long nap
- Take a walk and enjoy the scenery
- Watch cartoons and indulge with some snacks
- What the heck, just do them all!

Seldom do we let go of those busy, stressful days that engulf our lives. Far too often we abuse ourselves. We find time for others and never give time for self. Taking care of self should not be a challenge but a priority. Give yourself some added self-love. You can even title it a *Me Day*. This will mean taking in a day with no stresses, no worries, and no undue pressures. Pick any day of the week. It doesn't matter what day you choose, just pick. You deserve it, and self will love you for it—physically, emotionally, mentally, and spiritually. Enjoy it, and have a beautiful *Me Day!*

Complete this information after taking a "Me Day."

What date and day did you choose?

What did you do to nurture yourself on this day?

How did it feel to have a "Me Day?"

How often will you do a "Me Day" (i.e., daily, weekly, or monthly)?

What will you do on your next "Me Day?" (This could be more than one activity.)

3

Why Journal...Writing About Your Journey

Journeys: we all must take them! And when we do, there are lessons to be learned along the way. It is through these experiences one can learn to find self, discover the ability to forgive, build awareness, acquire first-hand knowledge, and gain personal growth. Life is about the hardships we face, the struggles we endure, and the challenges we overcome. Life is so full of stuff—the good, the bad, and the toxic. Through all that stuff, everyday life teaches us a new experience. Knowing that life brings on such beauty gives meaning to living!

Journaling is an art with a slew of synonyms—journal writing, journalizing, expressive writing, therapy writing, diary keeping. Those of us who haven't journaled before may be unaware of the beauty in journaling. When we take on the journal process, we're reaching into an emotional and physical pipeline to wellness. Look at journaling as a vehicle used to express emotions and a means to step into the past, present, and future. Be yourself, accept yourself, forgive yourself, and above all love yourself as you proceed through this guide of removing toxicity from your life! That's part of taking a journey and living.

Reasons for Journaling

Journaling is a great self-teaching vehicle! It functions as a private space of comfort and solace from the crazy world. It represents one's most genuine moments, shines on the ability to write, and digs deeper into one's feelings that may be difficult to voice aloud. Think of journaling as a reflector tool or a sounding board.

Journaling is a beautiful process as a healing medium. Beginning to journal is like expressively breaking through barriers and releasing the toxicants. Consider it a wound-healing process that nurtures the body and mind—physically, mentally, and emotionally. Journal writing is an exercise associated with therapy work.

Journaling . . . a completely free space to let loose inner thoughts, nurture wounds, track experiences and symptoms, gauge changes in mood or thought patterns, and reflect on feelings and emotions. It provides a look into the past, present, and future, as well as a soothing safe haven where one can redefine beliefs and values. It is a great way to harness one's creativity.

Everyone has their own opinion as to why journaling is beneficial. Thinking out of the box, how many reasons can you list?

Getting Ready to Journal
Mediums for Journaling

Plenty of options are available for journal-keeping. What works for you may not swing it for another. Anything you can use to record your thoughts will work. Besides a paper notebook, what are some other mediums for journaling? Don't forget about technology—there are even journaling apps.

Preparing to Write

When sitting down to record in a journal, whatever you choose for your medium, there's no need to worry about correct grammar or sentence structure. However, you will need to take into account:

- Finding a secluded place to write (i.e., a calm environment).

- Being committed to writing (i.e., making it a practice).

- Scheduling a writing time (i.e., staying consistent).

- Knowing what happened on a particular day (i.e., awareness).

Take a moment and consider what you need to do for starting a journal. What medium will you use? Do you have a good place to write where you can freely ponder your emotions? Write down how you're preparing to journal, paying special attention to the four points in the "Preparing to Write" section.

What to Write

Take a stab at starting your first journal entry. If you have already decided on your medium for journaling, write your first entry there. If you haven't acquired your chosen medium for journaling, record it on the page provided in this guide and then copy it into your journal when you get it.

When you start the entry, include the date. Consider providing your name, occupation, and things you like (doing this makes it personalized). If you like, include where you are writing, what time of day it is, or your current mood. Including these simple details will help get the writing juices flowing for when you need to write about the big stuff.

I can't tell you what to write . . . that's your call. For me, writing was and is a powerful tool for healing and releasing emotional pain. Get into your mind and thoughts, push them through, and let them flow. The deeper your feelings the better (this could be helpful too for writing purposes). Your entries should be as though you're talking to someone, such as a trusted friend. Again, try to be precise in remembering the details of your day—the scenes, emotions, attires, sounds, facial expressions, and any other particulars.

Journaling will feel more natural and enjoyable as you do it consistently. Don't fret if you miss a day or two or three or four—just continue with the current day's entry. Any events you've missed are bound to resurface if they are significant. When that happens, you'll be able to jot down the experience. Find a safe place to keep and secure your journal from others' viewing.

Remember, having a journal is like embracing a best friend—and one who knows how to keep all your secrets. For a quick practice, write about everything you've experienced on this particular day. Try to recall the entire day in detail—what was worn (by you or any others), your food intake, and your emotions. Did anything happen to stress you out? How did you handle a particular relationship? Are you going through some emotional pain?

READY, SET, GO!

Example journal outline

DAISY, MY SECRET JOURNAL *(Sample Name)*
Occupation: Nurse
Favorites: Cooking / Reading / Singing

Day:
Date:
Time: a.m. / p.m. *(Optional: Location)*:

How was that last exercise? Hopefully you found it refreshing, interesting, enriching, enlightening, soothing, calming, and fulfilling. Usually, the first journaling experience is challenging, yet rewarding.

4

Emotional Wellness and Toxic Emotions

Emotional wellness is a lifetime process. Don't think there's a quick fix! You may want to say, "I've done my part for emotional wellness. Now I can move on to something a bit more challenging." That's not the process for occupying the space of wellness. When it comes to emotional wellness, it's about dealing with life struggles and obstacles on a daily basis. The manner in which you embrace life's difficulties is a vital part of maintaining wellness.

If one's emotion is on a downward spiral, it's time for a self check-up. We seldom have time to take stock of our emotions. Understanding the elements, thoughts, feelings, and behaviors requires paying attention. Those elements are the makeup of our external and internal world. Emotions play a vital role in survival. One needs to be able to recognize what is a positive emotion and what is a negative emotion. Certain emotions can be positive or negative depending on the context.

Compile a list of negative emotions/feelings and their opposite for positive emotions/feelings.

Almost all negative emotions can be considered toxic when they result in violence or abuse against another person. Some of the most toxic emotions are anger, hate, and rage. Pick two toxic emotions from your list and draw what they might look like in a picture format and color in the emotions. Then pick two positive emotions and draw/color them. What differences do you see between the drawings?

Taking the necessary steps to get to a healthy level of emotional wellness should not be a chore or bring on frustration. One must embrace it as a necessity. Happiness and wellness make for good bed partners. Staying happy is the bedspread for protecting one's wellness. The best way to stay happy and emotionally well is by avoiding toxic emotions.

What Does Toxic Emotion Look Like?

Toxic emotion is a negative force that cuts completely through the body and mind, totally swallowing one up. It gnaws away until the person is stressed and emotionally drained. In a nutshell, it's a poison erupting within the body.

We all have built-in toxic emotions. Some of us suppress them. Others release them as soon as they feel them. Either way, these emotions explode like a bomb when released. By being aware of what we are feeling, we can de-escalate our toxic emotions and replace them with positive emotions.

One way to be aware of toxic emotions is to acknowledge that no one is baggage free. Everyone has a form of emotional baggage. Such baggage is a common cause of toxic emotions and can come from a divorce, a death, or a painful childhood memory. These traumatic events cause an upwelling of negative emotions. In addition to traumatic events, what are other scenarios where toxic emotions originate?

Emotions and Feelings

Although emotions and feelings seem interchangeable, there is a difference. Emotions are our reactions to external elements. Feelings are internal elements triggered by an emotion. For example, if someone jumps out and scares you, scared is the emotion and fear is the feeling triggered by that emotion.

On my journey to emotional wellness, I discovered an array of toxic emotions and feelings that had held me captive in a dark place for many years. As I pushed away from those unhealthy emotions/feelings, I needed to replace them with positive ones:

- **Hate** to be replaced with *Love*

- **Pain** to be replaced with *Joy*

- **Depression** to be replaced with *Resilience*

- **Guilt** to be replaced with *Innocence*

- **Rage** to be replaced with *Kindness*

Think a moment to recall an unhealthy relationship. Visualize this relationship in your mind or write down a brief description of it, focusing on the ugly and raw emotions and feelings that you felt while with this person. Afterward, close your eyes and visualize those unhealthy elements floating inside your circle. Literally push those unhealthy emotions away from you with your hand. What are you going to replace them with? Now, visualize these new positive emotions deleting all trace of the negative emotions. When you open your eyes, list those emotions and feelings you've pushed away and what they were replaced with. It may be easier to draw the experience with colors.

Controlling Toxic Emotions

A change in one's thinking process is essential for controlling toxins. When you notice negative feelings or emotions, replace them with positive thoughts as soon as possible! Built-up toxins are harmful and take a toll on the body, causing a drastic breakdown of the immune system. Be accountable for your actions and stand true to what you do and who you are. Just as you are what you eat, you are also what you think. If one continuously consumes unhealthy food, the body becomes unhealthy. If one always feeds into a negative thought pattern, the body processes the negative way of living. Those negative thoughts dictate the person you become.

Constantly being in a state of depression, anger, or hate directs the body to alter its immune system. Unhealthy emotions can cause illnesses. Holding on to those ugly emotions hinders spiritual growth and the ability to move forward in life. Stress has become a common factor of how a toxic emotion impacts the body. When we gain the knowledge to control our emotions, we've acquired power.

An excellent way to release built-up toxic emotions is through forgiveness. It can be difficult to forgive. It is hard to turn the other cheek when you've been slapped over and over. It takes a bigger you to walk away or be willing to forgive the person that has brought you the hurt and pain. There is power and healing in forgiveness.

One can learn to f_ _ _ _ _ _ although they may never f _ _ _ _ _ _.
F _ _ _ _ _ _ _ _ _ _ is the path to wellness.
F _ _ _ _ _ _ _ _ _ is also the prescription that wards off toxic emotions and feelings.
B _ true to yourself.
To a _ _ is wisdom. To have k _ _ _ _ _ _ _ _ is power.

Describe below an incident when you did not control a toxic emotion(s) from erupting. Was forgiveness a necessary part of overcoming the toxicity? If so, explain.

5

Young Adults Dating-N-Violence

This section has a great deal to offer for adolescents (ages 13 to 17) and young adults (ages 18 to 25). We become young adults before maturing to a full-fledged adult. Don't think young adults are not experiencing abuse—they are! Violence in the dating lifestyle of our young adults is a huge problem. They experience the same level of abuse as adults. Unhealthy relationships occur when one partner exercises control over the other. How would you define dating violence?

Living healthy is an essential part of one's lifestyle. Teaching our youth to make healthy choices in their tender years is just as vital. Consider this a wake-up call: Parents and educators, *we need to think about our young adults and strive to provide them with a healthier lifestyle.*

Poor habits exhibited by adults can be seen as a normal way of life to youth and young adults. These unhealthy habits jeopardize growth and the ability to function inside healthy relationships. We need to educate young adults by teaching them how to replace bad habits with good ones, starting with doing so in our own lives. This education promotes the disengagement of an unhealthy habit and reveals how bad habits jeopardize personal growth and one's ability to function inside healthy relationships. Teach both by word and example that unhealthy behaviors feed off negativity and maintaining wellness in one's life should be a priority. This will help young adults to make wiser choices when embarking on and engaging in relationships. If we teach them early on to make healthy decisions, living healthy becomes a valued part of their lifestyle. These young people will then recognize violence at face value and understand it has no place in society or their relationships.

With this awakening, they will learn abusers are creatures of habit and seldom change. It's important to know abuse is not just an act of physical behavior. The abuser can forcefully strip his or her victim of their emotional and mental energy. At this point, the victim becomes incapable of protecting self. They become prisoners, trapped and caged in their own environment. Being victimized is not an emotional place for happiness and doesn't offer room for mental growth. Getting away from the abuser is like a bird being released from its cage. After gaining a taste of freedom, there's no going back.

How can you help young adults become aware of violence in dating?

The interviews below of people all ages were conducted by the author to get their insight on violence in dating.

Lililiketheflower, the artist from Georgia

What are your thoughts on Young Adults Dating-N-Violence?

Lililiketheflower: It starts in your teen years when you're dating. When you go into dating and start off in an abusive and toxic situation, you get used to it. You begin to think that's how it's supposed to be. You think it's the norm and you accept that feeling . . . that it's what you deserve. It gets really hard to pull yourself away from it all, the longer you stay in there.

Were you ever caught up in it [toxic environment]?

L: I was young and grew up in an abusive household. So that was just kinda where it all started. It becomes the norm and you don't realize what a healthy relationship is supposed to look like. And when you're in an unhealthy relationship, it's hard to notice that it's not real love. It's simply just not real!

Do you think growing up in an abusive environment affected your adult lifestyle?

L: Yes, you carry that until you decide that's enough. I don't want this anymore, and I deserve better. You realize that you're worth much more. It's all about self-love and self-worth. Until then, you're going to allow people to treat you as bad as you treat yourself. So when you treat yourself better, you're not gonna allow people to treat you badly anymore.

How has it been for you in the dating arena?

L: It was toxic for a long time. I stayed in that toxic environment for five years. I was seventeen years old and ended it when I was twenty-two years old. I'm still having a hard time. Yes, a very hard time healing and really growing from that. Not allowing my past to affect my current relationships and the ability to move forward. Trauma, that's still a blockage and causing me to not fully be able to embrace who I have, now.

How did you end it?

L: I just didn't have a choice. I had to walk away from it. I realized that I didn't love myself by staying in the midst of toxicity. And that if I chose to stay, I was neglecting my health. So, that's why I knew I had to leave!

Coopie from Wisconsin

What thoughts would you care to share about Young Adults Dating-N-Violence?

Coopie: Every morning, be thankful and grateful. Love yourself first before you love anyone else. Having faith and having confidence in self is vitally important. Just be yourself always, and do some self-reflection. Know your aura is safe, calm, and clean from negativity.

Swapna from Georgia

What thoughts would you care to share about Young Adults Dating-N-Violence?

Swapna: Our children grow up too fast and they need to enjoy a childhood to face the world . . . and prepare for their responsibilities ahead.

Beth from Georgia

What thoughts would you care to share about Young Adults Dating-N-Violence?

Beth: My sister had a very personal experience with this in her teen years. Beyond any doubt it can mold an individual—make a person stronger or drive a person to one bad relationship after another. It tarnishes one's capability to not only seek out a healthy relationship, but [also] diminishes any hope of that person being a fulfilling partner to someone else. First and foremost, parental involvement is the *key*. Communication is everything, in any relationship. It's like a person who never goes to the doctor because they don't want to know if anything is wrong. The sooner we let go of the fear of the unknown, the truer we can be to what is actually going on in our lives.

The statements above add a real-life aspect to the dangers of toxic relationships and reminded me of my own experiences with violence in dating as a young adult. It took years before I rediscovered who I was, where I should be, or needed to be, in this life. If I had to relive it again, I would do things very differently—most of it, anyway. Mine was a lesson learned through the school of hard knocks. My journey began in those tender years, like so many others. Once I took a step into that unhealthy relationship as a mistress, my toxic world really started. Instead of stepping out of the imprint, I continued to walk deeper into its pathway. My life became one toxic experience after another. By the time I'd gotten through all that mess, I was emotionally, mentally, physically, and spiritually torn up. And that's all it was—a bunch of mess. For me, that dark world was a home for many years.

After reading the interviewees' responses and my own experience, what message would you share with others about violence in young adult relationships?

> *Young adults seem to drive in the fast lane, skipping the benefits of their stage of life in their rush to become full-fledged adults. Life has so much to offer them in their tender years. There's a lot to learn and know before transitioning into the full-fledged adult stage.*

Behavior of Violence

Violence is defined as actions or behaviors that inflict physical, sexual, mental, verbal, or emotional harm (i.e., abusive behavior) on another. All types of harm are forms of abuse. Violence between adults often originates from experiences incurred as young adults or children. The abuse experienced when younger becomes directed at another person as an adult. Violence in any relationship has damaging consequences. Listed below are the types of abuse. Next to it, list what that type of abuse could look like and its consequences. Feel free to list other forms of abuse as well.

Forms of Abuse	What Abuse Looks Like	Consequences of Abuse
Physical		
Sexual		
Mental		
Verbal	Put downs, belittling	Low self-esteem, mental scars
Emotional		

Standing Up to Dating-N-Violence

Take action against violence when you witness it in young adults or adult relationships. Refer to the list of red flags in Sections 6 and 7 and become familiar with them. It takes only *one* person to bring the red flags to someone's attention and possibly help them escape from a toxic relationship. What are some ways you can stand up to dating violence? A sample has been provided.

- Help someone see how they are being abused

After brainstorming some ways to help, consider these final two questions. Choose to write about the one that resonates with you (or write about both!).

1) Give a step-by-step process of how you'd assist a young adult involved in an abusive relationship.

2) Write about an unhealthy relationship you or someone close to you encountered as a young adult. Include how you/they managed to leave the relationship and lessons learned from them.

In any relationship, no partner should dictate what to wear, who to see, or who to associate with. You are your own person and you have rights. Above all, you have power and are in control! You need to exercise that power by using the word no. If you are committed to change, you have the ability to change. So make a change!

6
Signs of Being Toxic

Toxic relationships occur in society when two or more people interact in a way that is detrimental to their lives. But toxicity doesn't have to be people-related. A toxic relationship appears anytime there is an unhealthy action. Binge eating may indicate a toxic relationship between you and food, or you and your body.

Red Flags

These are a few identifying flags to help recognize an unhealthy interaction with someone:

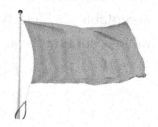

a) Extremely arrogant

b) Moves around / track record

c) Jealous

d) Blood sucker

e) Always negative

f) Liar

g) Abusive

h) Plays the victim

Match the flags above with a description below:

___ everybody's wrong and they're the type that knows it all

___ loves to drain your energy

___ honesty is only important when convenient

___ always a reason why moving from place to place

___ verbal, mental, and physical put downs

___ nothing is ever good enough; never seeing the positive side

___ always asking others to give of themselves

___ overly protective

Spotting Toxic People

Toxic people come in all forms, shapes, sizes, races, and genders . . . creating drama. Their toxicity generates an infestation that takes over their life and the lives of those around them. The damaging effect of their character hinders happiness and growth. It is crucial to recognize toxicity to avoid getting caught in the infestation.

What signs aid in spotting toxic people? These are indicators of a toxic, dysfunctional, and unhealthy person. Bullet points are acceptable to identify these signs. Some examples include having no regard for another's boundaries and being drama kings/queens.

Removing Toxic People

If someone is hindering your growth, then you're interacting with toxicity. Go ahead and slice that damaging relationship out of your circle. Think of it as cutting mold out of a contaminated piece of bread. Do you know a toxic person? If you don't, one is bound to cross your path . . . sooner, rather than later. These toxic people drain the life out of you with negative behaviors. Toxicity is contagious, insidious, and dangerous. With this knowledge, identify how toxic people affect you and why you need to remove them from your circle.

One cannot survive a healthy lifestyle clinging to toxic relationships . . . let them go! Having lived a life filled with toxicity and its poisons for many years, I know the crippling effects it leaves behind. So recognize and become aware! When someone you love unmasks their true colors, cut them from your circle.

7
Relationships from All Angles

For this section, we're going to take a look at your relationships from various angles. Being able to think critically about one's relationship is crucial! First, let's take a snapshot of your relationship and look inside.

One way to know what's going on is to see your relationship with fresh eyes. Fill in the chart below with the parts of your relationship that are working and the parts that aren't. Think carefully and honestly. Taking this approach allows the light of awareness to shine on a relationship, reveal its healthiness, show where it needs improvement, and highlight what makes it unhealthy or throws it in the danger zone.

The Positive Side of My Relationship	The Negative Side of My Relationship

Aha Moments

It's time for an aha moment! Aha moments occur when something that should be obvious to you but hasn't been suddenly becomes clear after a specific experience. The following scenarios were aha moments for various people realizing they were involved in an unhealthy or weak relationship. Do any of them sound familiar?

a) When I learned the money my partner kept asking for was being spent on another relationship.

b) When I learned my best friend loved to spend the night because he/she had been sleeping with my partner.

c) When I stayed up all night helping my partner study for an exam and he/she never thanked me.

d) When I denied my partner's accusation of being attracted to other men/women even though I am.

e) When I agreed with my partner's request to not tell anyone about when he/she slaps me.

List an aha moment you personally recall that involved a dysfunctional relationship. How did you handle the outcome of that aha moment?

Toxic Relationships

If one partner is toxic in a relationship, can the relationship continue being toxic without the toxic person? Of course not! That's because the toxic partner's behavior defines the relationship through control, manipulation, and power. Why does a non-toxic partner remain in an unhealthy or dysfunctional relationship? For that person, leaving becomes unimaginable or they hope to change the controller's behavior. Perhaps they feel their toxic partner is the only person to ever love them, their self-worth is dependent on their relationship with that person, or their controller's behavior does not change. In the long run, they may consider themselves a hostage of the relationship, conscious of the damage but unable to escape.

Once that toxic partner takes control, you may not realize you're in a toxic relationship or that you are a victim or even a hostage. Through varied dysfunctional activities, your partner has gained power and control over you. Take back the power you gave to that toxic partner. Don't become a prisoner to those who choose to control you. You can become your own worst enemy. No relationship is worth devaluing yourself. Empowerment is control, so empower yourself to be in control. Let go of the toxicity in your circle. Regain the power and break the chains of those who control you! When you've done that, the controller loses.

Don't become a victim! There are things you can do to let go of a toxic relationship. And it's not rocket science! Identify solutions you can use to render yourself free from an unhealthy partner-to-partner relationship. One idea is to empower yourself by physically leaving the presence of the toxic partner. After you've listed the varied approaches, write up an escape plan you would use to vacate an unhealthy environment. With this plan, lay out all the particular tools needed to gain your freedom. Think this out thoroughly as though it were an actual escape route.

Red Flags Part II

Sometimes the natural hunger for a mate causes us to get involved with an unhealthy person without realizing it. Do you
know there is a difference between being lonely and being des-
perate? Wake up, people! Eventually, the mask that toxic people
wear will come off, and those in a relationship with them will
suffer. Get real and stay aware.

Toxic relationships can appear inside your circle wearing more than one mask.
When that occurs, the two partners lack compatibility. One of them will be damaging
and unhealthy for the other. Their actions send a sign that warns **danger** to the other
partner if that partner is aware. Those red flags or signals indicate that the relationship
is seriously broken down, tainted, or damaged.

Listed below are some scenarios that are symptoms of unhealthy relationships. As
you read them, think of your relationship with a specific person—the scenarios refer to a
partner, but you could analyze your relationship with a parent, friend, or coworker. Can
you relate to the scenarios below? Put a check mark next to the scenario if you can relate
to any part of it.

a) Your partner always has an excuse why they need to go out. You have caught your
partner cheating and your partner tells you it will "never happen again."

b) When you question your partner about a particular situation, they answer with
something you know to be a lie.

c) Your partner has hit you and has an excuse for hitting you (like blaming you for
making him/her hit you).

d) Your partner always has to have the last word. Your partner outlines your
weaknesses in front of others (children, friends, colleagues).

e) Your partner frequently calls you names, particularly in front of others.

f) Your partner feels you're not spending enough time with them.

g) Your partner controls whom you speak to or socialize with. Your partner isolates
you from family and friends. Your partner listens in on calls or frequently checks
your call log.

h) Your partner consistently complains about his/her problems and never seems to have a good day. In general, he/she is a big whiner.

i) Your partner thinks life is so unfair and sees everything negatively.

j) Your partner lets an argument escalate and reacts physically without hurting you, like punching walls or breaking things.

The more checks you've marked, the more sour your relationship is. Whenever you can identify red flags in a relationship, you are empowered to get out of that unhealthy relationship, whether it involves a serious talk with your partner where you bring up your concerns or involving the authorities to assist. It's never too late to make that move to disconnect. When you do, you're on the right track! Think about the long-term effects on your emotional well-being if you continued your involvement with a partner who fits any of the descriptions above. Even a slight taste of unhealthiness can be dangerous and damaging on your psyche.

Categorize the descriptions above into the types of toxic partners listed below. Consider the first one as an example.

Abusive: c

Bitchy:

Cheater:

Controlling:

Dragger:

Explosive:

Jealous:

Liar:

Manipulator:

Negative:

> *Taking the steps to get back to self-love should never be ignored. Stay attentive to those red flags. When they surface, run as fast as you can . . . find a safe haven and get the heck out of there!*

Crazy Mind Games

In many relationships, people (regardless of gender) tend to play crazy mind games. What do these mind games look like? Like mixed signals! The person will say one thing and totally mean something different, which toys with our emotions, feelings, and mind. Whether it's a partner, family, or friend, we get caught up in their game playing. When this happens, we spin our wheels trying to figure out their angle. This can become very irritating, exhausting, and frustrating when it comes to building meaningful relationships. When we find ourselves scraping and scrambling to survive inside the relationship, it's time to make a decision. How would you start an honest conversation that eliminates the tricks or mind games?

Games can be exciting and fun when intended for the sole purpose they were designed—as games. Sometimes the brain needs a little stimulation the fun way. Try your hand at this mind game! Unscramble the words to know which ones to eliminate from the list at the bottom. The first one shows an example, and any word with a hyphen in the list will not include the hyphen in the scramble. Go for it!

oollhca a l c o h o l

cpeentealccsaf _ _ _ _ _ _ _ _ _ _ _ _ _ _

wderivwlo _ _ _ _ _ _ _ _ _

plasfcmnoiosse _ _ _ _ _ _ _ _ _ _ _ _ _

feofrsvslieegsn _ _ _ _ _ _ _ _ _ _ _ _ _ _

yojaeusl _ _ _ _ _ _ _ _

ahptwya _ _ _ _ _ _ _

roynjeu _ _ _ _ _ _ _

seanearws _ _ _ _ _ _ _ _ _

inootmale _ _ _ _ _ _ _ _ _

glnyi _ _ _ _ _

tcopnces _ _ _ _ _ _ _ _

rgthuni _ _ _ _ _ _ _

tnaiseles _ _ _ _ _ _ _ _ _

feosllve _ _ _ _ _ _ _ _

gtitinh _ _ _ _ _ _ _

rpae _ _ _ _

limefasi _ _ _ _ _ _ _ _

grdsu _ _ _ _ _

tnoiloista _ _ _ _ _ _ _ _ _

iuerbtnpl _ _ _ _ _ _ _ _ _

sbaue _ _ _ _ _

smuror _ _ _ _ _ _

estefeelms _ _ _ _ _ _ _ _ _ _

looctnr _ _ _ _ _ _ _

dpsnwotu _ _ _ _ _ _ _ _ _

ltiueqias _ _ _ _ _ _ _ _ _

gttxein _ _ _ _ _ _ _ _

fneidrlgir _ _ _ _ _ _ _ _ _ _

poinsreesd _ _ _ _ _ _ _ _ _ _

arfe _ _ _ _

sgltinak _ _ _ _ _ _ _ _

tfeeylsil _ _ _ _ _ _ _ _ _

nsensoidmi _ _ _ _ _ _ _ _ _ _

fcndnlfeeeoisc _ _ _ _ _ _ _ _ _ _ _ _ _ _

tcdeiandoi _ _ _ _ _ _ _ _ _ _

glasnechle _ _ _ _ _ _ _ _ _ _

srpsihlanitoe _ _ _ _ _ _ _ _ _ _ _ _ _

rtmetnate _ _ _ _ _ _ _ _ _

tsrolwfeh _ _ _ _ _ _ _ _ _

vssodiicree _ _ _ _ _ _ _ _ _ _ _

aisrtt _ _ _ _ _ _

ctiox _ _ _ _ _

nnipatiaoulm _ _ _ _ _ _ _ _ _ _ _ _

retaprn _ _ _ _ _ _ _

haylthe _ _ _ _ _ _ _

enoleivc _ _ _ _ _ _ _ _

miictv _ _ _ _ _ _

dticoemmt _ _ _ _ _ _ _ _ _

etrdpsices _ _ _ _ _ _ _ _ _ _

repwo _ _ _ _ _

gfdelcnite _ _ _ _ _ _ _ _ _ _

elopep _ _ _ _ _ _

rnogw _ _ _ _

abuse, acts, ~~alcohol~~, assets, awareness, betrayal, biting, blueprint, breakdown, caught, challenges, cheating, committed, constant, concepts, control, couples, crossroads, dedication, deflecting, defining, depression, dimensions, discoveries, disrespect, divorce, drugs, escalating, endearing, energy, emotional, essential, establish, family, families, fear, fights, forms, girlfriend, grabbing, grow, healthy, hitting, hurting, isolation, jealousy, journey, kind, life, lifestyle, lying, manipulation, monitoring, months, mutual, partner, pathway, people, period, pets, pointers, power, punching, putdowns, qualities, rape, relationships, roots, rumors, scratching, self-acceptance, self-compassion, self-confidence, self-esteem, self-forgiveness, self-love, self-worth, shaking, singles, slapping, smoking, stalking, STDs, strangers, suicide, support, tech, texting, threats, throwing, things, toxic, traits, treatment, verbal, victim, violence, worldwide, worships

8
Toxicity in the Workplace

Toxicity in the workplace is common. When picking a workplace, look for an environment that is strong and healthy. Sometimes even a healthy workplace can become an unhealthy, toxic environment.

Unless we have our own business, co-workers or supervisors are inherited. And within that group, someone is bound to spew their venom. Can you survive in toxicity? Sure, survival is possible in a tainted and damaging world. One can be very successful and productive working among those toxins. That's because knowledge is p _ _ _ _ !

Write about or draw a toxic experience you or someone you know encountered in the workplace. Who was the toxic person? How did you or the person you know handle the poison coming from that toxic person? If the situation was handled well, what went well? If the situation wasn't handled well, what would have improved it?

The Promotion
Imagine this . . .

You have an offer to be a Health Safety and Environmental Coordinator for company XYZ. Your mission is to ensure all employees have a safe and healthy environment. For many employees, dealing with the toxicity of a couple of colleagues has been a major issue. What techniques are you going to implement to make your office a healthier workplace? There are no limits to what you can do. Some ideas include coaching classes to identify toxic behaviors or a zero-tolerance policy for those behaviors exhibited by the toxic colleagues.

Curing the Toxins

One toxic person in the workplace is quite enough . . . even that one person needs to go! Negative entities, with their dependent traits and selfishness, love sucking the life out of another. They are poisonous people, spewing their venoms throughout the workplace. Their poison hinders others from living a healthy lifestyle. Staying free of toxic relationships is not easy. Change is necessary to cut toxins out of your life and circle. Think of toxic relationships like an oil spill in the ocean. The damage it causes is life-threatening and immediate action needs to be taken to protect yourself.

With the proper tools, you can survive the toxins. In case those toxins find their way into your path and spew their poison at you, here are a few simple cures:

a) Exit and get the heck out of there

b) Ignore, ignore, ignore to block out those deadly toxins

c) Maintain professionalism (don't feed off the poison)

d) Establish boundaries

e) Keep complete control of your own emotions

f) Build an immune system to counteract (that unhealthy side of living)

g) Maintain a positive mindset

h) Don't take it personally (many abusers are wounded themselves)

Next to the choices below, place the correct alphabet from above to coincide to its cure. The first set has been completed.

_d_ take control; at all cost limit communication

___ toxic people need serious help; don't take ownership of one's issue

___ it's hard to knock a positive; filter through to others

___ the positive outweighs the negative; keep character intact; limit being sucked in

___ learn to tune out the snake with their venom; don't be a part of their show

___ less chance of stealing one's joy

___ a toxic person is contagious; there's the risk of becoming contaminated

___ self-esteem builds up; become the bigger of the two

Signs in the Workplace

We've discussed toxic red flags in Sections 6 and 7, but let's focus on signs of toxicity in the workplace. To be cognizant of toxicity, one has to know how it appears. Here are some signals to watch for inside the workplace:

1) Bullies

2) Selfishness

3) Liars

4) One person is always the victim

5) Lack of kindness

6) Full of drama

7) Negative office environment

8) Cruel to others

9) Busybodies

10) Unappreciative

11) Always have to be right

12) Health suffers

Next to the choices below, place a corresponding number from above that completes the triggered signs.

___ careless of others' needs or feelings

___ deliberately misleading and tends to twist information

___ unless it serves their purpose and needs

___ loves pity parties and refuses to let go of things even magnifies situations

___ about anything and blames others

___ always about self

___ in a ruckus or chaos and morale diminishes

___ always talking down to others

___ continuously blaming others and not self

___ always minding other people's business

___ never wrong about anything and knows all about everything

___ mentally, physically, or emotionally

> *Recognizing a toxic **red flag** is the first step in bringing light to a world of darkness. You've heard of miracles? Miracles do happen! Our Creator brought me from the darkness into the light. He will do the same for you. There's nothing our Creator can't do!*

9

Combating Abuse and Violence

Abuse and violence may seem interchangeable, but understand their views are different. Violence is a specific type of abuse that involves physical harm. One person may abuse another without violence. Abuse takes on a variety of shapes and forms (e.g., mental, emotional, physical, economical, etc.) but always the abuser seeks to take control over another. When this occurs, there is an imbalance of power between the abuser and victim. Acts of violence or abuse are not limited to criminals—the violator can live next door or be a family member. Any form of abuse is damaging to the level it causes the victim to devalue and doubt self. The abuser can then readily take control over his or her victim. It's important to know abuse and violence are choices, as are our responses to that abuse or violence.

In this section, readers will familiarize themselves with levels of abuse and violence and the various forms of how they are revealed. It's known that abuse occurs when one hurts another. Since the perpetrator doesn't wear an abusive "name tag," forms of abuse can be hard to identify. To get our creative minds connected with this topic, think of some other words you associate with abuse (similar to Section 1 when we identified the faces of toxicity). It may help to reflect on times when you've seen or experienced abuse or violence.

Identifying Types of Abuse and Violence

Next, you'll find an incomplete list of many forms of abuse and violence. For each, fill in the blanks and circle its type. In order to be able to stand against abuse and violence, you have to be able to identify each. Beneath each type, define it and what it looks like when it's happening. A few of the answers have been filled in to give you an idea.

Ne _ _ _ _ _ (abuse or violence or neither)
Is when: someone is responsible for providing adequate care or assistance but doesn't.
And looks like: having no regard for one's daily living necessities; abandonment; failure to give attention to medical or physical needs.

Financial (abuse or violence)
Is when: someone takes control over another's financial possessions without consent.
And looks like: taking funds from another to use for personal gain; doesn't give free access to money; gives an allowance; makes list and angers when list is deviated from.

Se _ _ _ _ (abuse or violence)
Is when:
And looks like:

Di _ _ _ _ (abuse or violence)
Is when: technology is used to intimidate another.
And looks like:

Ps _ _ _ _ _ _ _ _ _ _ (abuse or violence)
Is when:
And looks like:

Cultural (abuse or violence)
Is when: act of mistreatment occurs due to one's beliefs or culture.
And looks like:

Sp _ _ _ _ ual (abuse or violence)

Is when:

And looks like:

Em _ _ _ _ _ _ _ (abuse or violence)

Is when:

And looks like: making one feel useless or invaluable.

Ve_ _ _ _ (abuse or violence)

Is when: hurtful remarks are spoken or written to one person.

And looks like:

Phy _ _ _ _ _ (abuse or violence)

Is when:

And looks like:

Setting Limits

Now that we've defined the forms of abuse and violence, consider how they are present in your life and the lives of those around you. It is vitally important to be accountable for our actions and acknowledge when our own actions are straying into violent/abusive behavior territory. One of the best ways to combat being abusive or violent is to make sure we, ourselves, are not perpetrators. Establishing boundaries is a great way to limit self from toxicity. Using the "and looks like" answers above, write down what your specific personal boundaries will be.

10
Healthy Is the New Me

Mirror, Mirror, Is that Me?

Look in a mirror and focus on yourself very closely. Look deep, deep, and deeper into the glass. Don't miss seeing a wrinkle, a mole, a pimple, a freckle, a hair, an eyelid, an earlobe, an expression, or an emotion that pops out at you. Be prepared to draw the image that appears. Hopefully, this is the person you've become. The brightness that shines through you will glimmer and reflect your change. You've spent a lot of time and energy acknowledging self, recapturing your life, who you are, and who you are becoming. There is so much that lives inside the inner you and no one should be able to rob you of that possession. Don't allow anyone to steal your joy, ever again. Keep growing and shining. You are so beautiful!

Draw or write about the person you've seen in the mirror. It's important to be real with yourself. If you were wearing a mask while looking through the glass, show that too. If there was a sour emotion or an ugly frown, don't leave it untold. Your picture should depict some form of color as well. Be precise in your details and don't worry about trying to be an artist.

Now that you've come this far, write out a character description of the *new you* living inside your healthy lifestyle. After letting go of the negative entities discussed previously, how does the *new you* treat self? What were some of the old things you've released to acquire this new part of self?

Taking the Challenge

In this challenge, you will be able to identify the new you in your relationships. After completing the exercise, consider how your answers may have changed from when you began this guidebook.

Circle the appropriate answer to complete this activity.

In our relationship, my partner

1) Is liked by most, if not all, of my friends. Yes / No

2) Is okay with me spending time with others. Yes / No

3) Is understanding when I see friends or go to activities without him/her. Yes/No

4) Has no problem validating my feelings. Yes / No

5) Has no problem with me having my own space when needed. Yes / No

6) Loves and embraces us spending quality time together. Yes / No

Any negative response is a **red flag** indicating you need to rethink the safety of your relationship. If that is the case, list what direction you'll move toward to make that change. This is all part of the process of becoming a new you! If your relationship is positive, write down how that makes you feel.

New Gifts

The new gifts you've acquired center on self-concepts (e.g., self-esteem, self-confidence, self-worth, self-reliance, etc.) and make a healthier and richer lifestyle. You have become a new person! A great way to maintain these newly realized gifts of self are to recognize your positive personality traits and how they bolster your sense of self.

1) What personal traits do you possess that strengthen self? What traits or habits do you have that you should let go of . . . to let self—the new you—shine?

2) How would you describe the old you? What lessons did you gain from being inside an unhealthy partner-to-partner relationship?

3) How would you describe the new you? What will you do differently to sustain a healthy lifestyle?

Acquiring self-knowledge brings awareness to all desires, needs, failures, and whatever else is necessary to become this new person. With the new you, there should be new thoughts, a new image, and a new attitude.

11

Living Safe Within My Circle

What does it take to live safely within one's own environment? That's the million dollar question! We are living in turbulent times. The news of the dangers of life is spread across the world through TV screens and newspapers. No one is safe—not on your commute, not in your own home, not at church. The evidence is in the mass killings. Not a day, hour, minute, or second passes without a life or lives being taken as a result of toxic interactions. There's no doubt this world is broken and crippled by toxicity. Toxicity is alive and active!

With the toxic interactions happening in today's world, we're all struggling to survive, to live a safer and healthier lifestyle. Love drives away toxicity. What does love mean to you, and how does love relate to safety? What does a safe world look like to you? In this description, lay it all out: people, diseases, environments, settings, emotions and feelings. Using your imagination, how would you color or draw that safe world?

Living safely is not only a matter of protecting yourself from outside elements but the inside ones as well. These questions will help you shed light on how safe and healthy you are living within your circle.

True or False: Circle or underline the answer you think is appropriate.

1) True or false: If a partner hits you out of frustration or anger and promises not to do it again, you should believe him/her.

2) True or false: Usually, the toxic signs don't appear until the third or fourth time in a relationship. Only after giving someone multiple chances can you really know the partner is an unhealthy mate.

3) True or false: It is easy to recognize abusive relationships because there are only four types.

4) True or false: It is okay if your partner's personality changes during the relationship since he/she is still the same person you fell in love with.

5) True or false: It is okay for your partner to use a form of abuse or addiction. It simply means he/she is feeling stressed, but the relationship is *not* in jeopardy.

6) True or false: Only women can be abused in a relationship.

7) True or false: When a partner says no to your advances, he/she doesn't really mean no.

8) True or false: To be physically violated is not as bad as being verbally or emotionally abused.

9) True or false: Having a drug/alcohol dependency to function doesn't affect the family as a whole.

10) True or false: There are limited treatment programs available for people with abuse issues.

11) True or false: Family members have no place getting involved with someone's substance abuse treatments.

12) True or false: The internet and cell phones are instruments for dating abuse.

13) True or false: Parents are good observers when it comes to their teen being abused.

14) True or false: In an unhealthy relationship, your partner doesn't respect your boundaries. He/she will use texting as a means to keep tabs on another to stay in control.

Signs of Unsafe Environment

People who live in undesirable communities are at a risk of experiencing negative interactions. Identify signs that indicate a place may not be safe. Try to think of as many signs as you can.

Examples include mass killings, defensive people, drug/alcohol abusers, and carjacking incidents. How would you draw that unsafe environment?

Degrees of Safety

The concept of safety encompasses a range of factors. This includes but is not limited to freedom from physical, sexual, and emotional abuse. The feeling of safety can result from the smallest and simplest things. Identify elements that help you feel safe. Think outside the box! Examples include listening to/talking with a dear friend, cozying up with a pillow or book, establishing boundaries, and clinging to religious beliefs.

Freeing toxic relationships from one's circle is not an easy task . . . but the end result is well worth it.

Royalty Treatment

Our home and the relationships we have should be places of safety. One way to make our home and relationships safe is by treating them the best we can. Think of your home as a castle, a place of serenity, peace, happiness, comfort, love, and care. Within those four walls reside a king and queen. It's okay to treat your partner like a king or queen as long as you don't lose yourself in the process. You are royalty, living inside the castle draped in all its beauty. You and your partner are refined, precious, and rare creations.

Just as we recognize our beauty and our worth and spend time cultivating self, we must allow our partner space to do the same. One must take care of self to enable care of another. Every king nurtures his queen and every queen nurtures her king. The beauty of nurturing varies from man to woman. Women may tend to be more expressive in their needs and desires than men. But that doesn't diminish the level of giving on either part. A partner should never lay a hand on another unless it's to nurture or caress in a comforting, romantic, or intimate setting. We are kings and queens and should strive to treat each other as such. Our treatment of one another should be respectful, genuine, attentive, decent, and kind.

As kings and queens, we strive to build an unbreakable and unshakable union. You are top priority to your partner just as he/she is to you. There is nothing that comes between the bonding. We each want to be cared for, appreciated, desired, respected, needed, understood, honored, and loved. Once you discover you are a VIP, a king or queen, embrace that moment. There is so much one can do to gratify and beautify a relationship when you realize the worth of your partner.

How would you draw and color your king/queen in all his/her glory? What type of royal treatment would you give him/her? You can use bullet points to outline the descriptive treatments. You have the magic touch to create the picture of this royal family (include little princes and princesses, if desired).

12

Living Healthy, Thinking Healthy, Being Healthy

Age is wisdom, knowledge is power! It takes a lot of work to build healthy relationships. Don't be discouraged as you take the journey toward self-love. That which is beautiful requires work. To obtain self is not an easy task.

You've made it this far to beautify your life, meaning you're doing the work to live a healthier lifestyle. It's up to you to maintain that healthy environment. Your self-love sends a message to the voiceless. Promise yourself to nurture the self-love living inside you.

Self-talk is an essential part of healthy living. Think with your head and not the heart. It's important to ask these questions of self: *Who am I? Do I really love me? Am I taking care of myself—emotionally, physically, mentally, and spiritually? Am I letting go of stressors?* These are important questions, particularly when you come out of a relationship. You'll need to give solid thought to your answers before allowing another into your life.

Remember, stay focused and sustain the goal to build self-love. Take baby steps to create habits of self-love. Believe in yourself. Self-discovery is such an amazing adventure! Now that you've started the journey, there's no turning back.

Relationship Agreement

No one deserves to be treated like a possession. Be real with yourself and others will have to learn to accept you. They will like you or they will dislike you—and either option is okay. We've been conditioned to see the beauty in others but not within ourselves. The person you are now will naturally grow and evolve to maintain self-love, self-worth, self-confidence, self-reliance, and self-esteem. Your sense of self will be the key to fulfilling relationships.

Another aspect of a successful relationship is the relationship agreement. Are you familiar with relationship agreements? Think of it as a means to cement the love in a relationship. These documents are not legally binding, but the symbolic binding of the agreement is priceless in its ability to strengthen relationships. There will be times when either party may get off track. That's part of being human. Don't sweat it or fret it! With tact, care, and love, use the guidelines to refocus. Move forward to embrace and honor the beauty expressed by those words.

Keep in mind: this form of connection helps partners to align their expectations and outlines the way partners want to be treated. It's a chance for each party to voice what they want and need from the relationship. Your wants and needs make you whole. As each partner is true to self, the other partner will understand one's true desires. Make a practice to ensure that self-love is a part of your wholeness diet and routine. *Your life will never be the same!*

On the next page, you will find an example relationship agreement with suggested form and verbiage. Following the example is an empty agreement you can tailor to your relationship. As you do so, stay attentive to being honest about wants, listening to each other, validating each other, and acknowledging that it will be a give-and-take situation within that relationship. The information inside the bullet points should contain an array of expectations.

As people change, re-examine and amend the contract as appropriate. You and your partner should set a specific time to look over the agreement, to ensure it meets the relationship's needs. Remember, you'll need to update the connected agreement with addendum items, as the need arises. It's about living healthy, thinking healthy, and being healthy!

Relationship Agreement

Dated: _____

Initiated by: _____

This relationship's agreement is entered into between _____ and _____. Its terms of conditions start on _____ and terminate on _____. Should we choose not to reestablish our connection upon its termination, this relationship shall part peacefully, lovingly, graciously, and respectfully with each partner free of any liabilities.

This is an agreement that nurtures a healthy relationship and is shared as partners. Let's give each other space to live to the fullest. With our love, this binding connection will be embraced, respected, and honored, accordingly:

We have the right to

- Ask to spend quality time with one another

- Be angry or happy

- Be treated and nurtured with dignity, respect, love, and care

- Explain our actions or behaviors (if we choose)

- Make decisions separate from the other

- Make friends without permission from the other

- Not relinquish any money to the other without reason

- Our own feelings and emotions, however they are expressed

- Our own free and honest opinion

- Our own free space

- Our privacy when talking on the phone

- Plan outings that nurture our relationship (emotionally, mentally, physically, and spiritually)

- Respectfully be heard

- Respectfully disagree

- Say no at any time

- Think for ourselves

We have the responsibility to

- Ask for help when it's needed

- Be respectful and expect the same from one another, as partners

- Be thoughtful in nurturing the relationship

- Set high expectations for the other

- Set limits and boundaries

- Strive to maintain a strong, healthy, and fulfilling environment

We shall make an effort to meet on equal grounds. We now look at the relationship from a brighter perspective and no longer participate in drama or negative interactions.

Relationship Agreement

Dated: _____ Ending: _____

Signed by _____and_____

The above parties commit to freely abide by this relationship agreement. In this relationship, we agree to meet the expectations outlined while maintaining a loving and nurturing connected force.

-
-
-
-
-
-
-
-
-
-
-
-
-
-

-
-
-
-
-
-
-
-

Henceforth, we're committed to growing and creating a valuable future with one another. Our utmost goal is to live up to its defined beauty. This agreement will be revised or renegotiated as deemed necessary.

Through My Own Eyes: Rediscovery

Suggested materials for this page: pencil/pen, colored pencils/crayons

You've been over many hurdles to get here.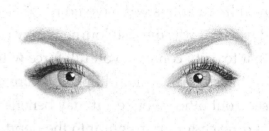
Taking care of self has never been easy. A lot
of nurturing goes into being a better you.
Consider your journey as a blueprint for a
life that's been beautified and enriched. This
new life offers a healthy way of living. With
all the discoveries made, it's time to take a second look. This vision you've acquired has
likely shifted your worldview. Hopefully, after reading, you've captured a refreshing
insight into how to be a better you. Surely you've conquered a greater passion for self.

How do you see the world now? Your drawing should depict a vision of your new
world. Remember—it's your world. No one can tell you how to live it but you! Let all
that hard work shine through your images. And be proud of who you have become.
Have fun and draw away!

Farewell for Now

I applaud you for taking steps to put yourself and your relationships in check by reading this Information/Success Guide. Hopefully you've gained an understanding that unhealthy relationships have no place in your circle. Tomorrow isn't promised. Live each day as if it was the last! Journeys may come and go, but memories are everlasting. Know that toxicity comes at you full force with its many disguises.

Sharing is caring. I hope you care enough to spread the word about this guide, or seek out others you feel it may benefit. Everyone should be eager to find their self-love and reach for an insight into the depth of toxicity. Any literary work makes for a great and unique gift!

Appendix A

More Ingredients

Here you can find a few resources to nourish your journey toward increased self-love. They are great reads for learning about toxic and tainted relationships and discovering inner love.

Freedom from Toxic Relationships: Moving on from The Family, Work and Relationship Issues That Bring You Down
by Avril Carruthers

Toxic relationships often come disguised as seemingly normal ones. These subtly destructive relationships are characterized by the slow erosion of self-esteem.

Toxic Relationships: How to Regain Lost Power in Your Relationship
by Kimberly J. Brasher

An eye-opening look at relationships in our lives that cause us pain and frustration either with a spouse, sibling, in-law, grandparent, or a controlling, toxic boss. How to take back control.

The 5 Love Languages: The Secret to Love That Lasts
by Gary Chapman

Keeping a relationship thriving means understanding how to speak the language that best suits your partner.

The Self-Esteem Workbook, Second Edition
by Glenn R. Schiraldi, PhD

Includes up-to-date information on brain plasticity, and new chapters on forgiveness, mindfulness, and cultivating self-esteem.

The Four Loves
by C.S. Lewis

Examines four varieties of human love: affection, the most basic form; friendships, the rarest and perhaps most insightful; Eros, passionate love; and charity, the greatest and least selfish.

The Gifts of Imperfection: Let Go of Who You Think You're Supposed to Be and Embrace Who You Are
by Brené Brown

Ten guideposts on the power of wholehearted living—a way of engaging with the world from a place of worthiness.

Radical Self Love: A Guide to Loving Yourself and Living Your Dream
by Gala Darling

Begin to discover exactly what makes you so magnificent, and uncover a litany of tools and techniques to love yourself.

Madly in Love with ME: The Daring Adventure of Becoming Your Own Best Friend
by Christine Arylo

This breakthrough book on self-love takes you beyond the idea of loving, valuing, and caring for yourself into something much deeper.

A Return to Love: Reflection on the Principles of "A Course in Miracles"
by Marianne Williamson

How we each can become a miracle worker by accepting God and by the expression of love in our daily lives.

Love Is Letting Go of Fear, Third Edition
by Gerald G. Jampolsky, MD

Both helpful and hopeful, this little gem of a guide offers twelve lessons to help us let go of the past and stay focused on the present.

Appendix B

In the News

New York City became the first major US city to tackle the issue of girls' self-esteem and body image.[1] Recognizing that girls at the ripe ages of six and seven years old struggle with body image and self-esteem was a remarkable breakthrough. This city launched a self-esteem initiative program that aids girls in acknowledging that their value is derived from character, skills, and attributes—and that awareness of appearance has little weight. This was a major development and great accomplishment for the city of New York.

- Over 80% of 10-year-old girls are afraid of being fat.[2]

- By middle school, 40-70% of girls are dissatisfied with two or more body parts. Body satisfaction hits rock bottom between ages 12-15.[3]

- Girls' self-esteem plummets at age 12 and doesn't improve till age 20.[4]

- An estimated 24 million people (i.e., up to 8% of U.S. population) suffer from anorexia, bulimia, or binge eating disorder, all triggered by "garden-variety" dieting.[5]

- Up to 4.2% of women suffer from anorexia, up to 40% experience bulimia, and 2.8% of American adults struggle with binge eating disorder.[6]

Bullying

- Obese children were 63% more likely to be bullied regardless of gender, race, family income, social skills, academic achievement, or school composition.[7]

- Girls with high self-esteem in seventh grade are three times more likely to keep their virginity than girls with low self-esteem.[8]

• The risk of teenage motherhood rises to 50% among (girl) teens with lower self-esteem.[9]

Obesity

• Young girls who dieted had three times the odds of becoming overweight five years later compared with girls not using weight-control behaviors.[10]

• People who feel discriminated or stigmatized against because of weight were two-and-a-half times more likely to become obese, regardless of their regular weight.[11]

Self-esteem with self-actualization equates to . . .

• A broad spectrum of growth

• A solid understanding of the self-concepts

• Lack of comparison to others

• High opinion of one's self

• Self-confidence

• Feelings of worthiness

• Reflecting one's own self-worth

• Fully developed abilities

The formula for self-esteem equates to successes measured by failures.

References

[1] NYC Girls Project. *About the New York City Girl's Project.* NYC Resources 311, Office of the Mayor. Retrieved from http://www.nyc.gov/html/girls

[2] Andrist, Linda C. "Media images, body dissatisfaction, and disordered eating in adolescent women." *American Journal of Maternal Child Nursing*, March/April 2003, 28(2): 119–123.

[3] Cash, Thomas, F., and Pruzinsky, Thomas. *Body Image: A Handbook of Theory, Research, and Clinical Practice.* New York: Guilford, 2002.

[4] Baldwin, Scott A., and Hoffmann, John P. "The dynamics of self-esteem: A growth-curve analysis." *Journal of Youth and Adolescence*, 31: 101–113.

[5, 6] "7 powerful statistics." Avalon Hills Foundation. February 2015. Retrieved from http://www.avalonhillsfoundation.org/blog/2015/02/7-powerful-statistics-about-eating-disorders/

[7] Puhl, Rebecca M., Petersen, Jamie Lee, and Luedicke, Joerg. "Weight-based victimization: Bullying experiences of weight loss treatment-seeking youth." *Pediatrics*, January 2013, 131(1): e1–e9.

[8, 9] Spencer, J. M., Zimet, Gregory D., Aalsma, Matthew C., and Orr, Donald P. "Self-esteem as a predictor of initiation of coitus in early adolescents." *Pediatric*, April 2002, 109(4): 581–584.

[9] Dennison, Catherine. "Teenage pregnancy: An overview of the research evidence." Nice.org, 2004. Retrieved from http://www.nice.org.uk/niceMedia/documents/teenpreg evidence overview.pdf

[10] Neumark-Sztainer, D., Wall, M., Guo, J., Story, M., Haines, J., and Eisenberg, M. "Obesity, disordered eating, and eating disorders in a longitudinal study of adolescents: How do dieters fare 5 years later?" *Journal of the American Dietetic Association*, 2006, 106(4): 559–568.

[11] Sutin, Angelina R., and Terracciano, Antonio. "Perceived Weight Discrimination and Obesity," *PLoS One*, July 2013, 8(7), e70048.

Remember, you always come first. Allow no one to steal your joy.

Take the time to nurture and care for yourself with lots of **self-love**.

You've achieved something totally remarkable, a new you.

Congratulations . . . You did it!

What do you say to toxic people? "Stay away from me. You're contagious!"

About the Author

Nina Norstrom is the author of *Not A Blueprint, It's the Shoe Prints that Matter: A Journey Through Toxic Relationships.* She is a requested speaker on the topic of toxic relationships and the havoc they can create in our lives.

According to Nina, "Life is about experiences (the good, bad, and the ugly) and the lessons they teach us. If we pay attention, a lot of insight is gained along the way."

Nina resides in the state of Georgia. As a dedicated and passionate champion, she lives an empowered lifestyle.